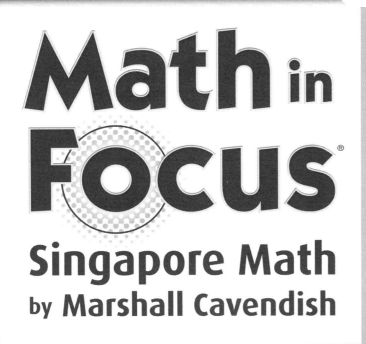

Enrichment

Consultant and Author
Dr. Fong Ho Kheong

Author
Ang Kok Cheng

US Distributor

© Copyright 2009, 2013 Edition Marshall Cavendish International (Singapore) Private Limited

Published by Marshall Cavendish Education
An imprint of Marshall Cavendish International (Singapore) Private Limited
Times Centre, 1 New Industrial Road, Singapore 536196
Customer Service Hotline: (65) 6411 0820
E-mail: tmesales@sg.marshallcavendish.com
Website: www.marshallcavendish.com/education

Distributed by
Houghton Mifflin Harcourt
222 Berkeley Street
Boston, MA 02116
Tel: 617-351-5000
Website: www.hmheducation.com/mathinfocus

First published 2009
2013 Edition

All rights reserved. Permission is hereby granted to teachers to reprint or photocopy in classroom quantities, for use by one teacher and his or her students only, the pages in this work that carry the appropriate copyright notice, provided each copy made shows the copyright notice. Such copies may not be sold, and further distribution is expressly prohibited. Except as authorized above, no part of this publication may be reproduced, stored in a retrieval system or transmitted, in any form or by any means, electronic, mechanical, photocopying, recording or otherwise, without the prior written permission of Marshall Cavendish Education.

Marshall Cavendish and *Math in Focus* are registered trademarks of Times Publishing Limited.

Math in Focus® Enrichment 1A
ISBN 978-0-669-01574-4

Printed in Singapore

1 2 3 4 5 6 7 8 1897   18 17 16 15 14 13
4500346045   A B C D E

Contents

CHAPTER 1 Numbers to 10 — 1

CHAPTER 2 Number Bonds — 9

CHAPTER 3 Addition Facts to 10 — 19

CHAPTER 4 Subtraction Facts to 10 — 26

CHAPTER 5 Shapes and Patterns — 33

CHAPTER 6 Ordinal Numbers and Position — 42

CHAPTER 7 Numbers to 20 — 51

CHAPTER 8 Addition and Subtraction Facts to 20 — 59

CHAPTER 9 Length — 66

Answers — 75

Introducing Math in Focus® Enrichment

Written to complement *Math in Focus®: Singapore Math by Marshall Cavendish* Grade 1, exercises in *Enrichment 1A* and *1B* are designed for advanced students seeking a challenge beyond the exercises and questions in the Student Books and Workbooks.

These exercises require children to draw on their fundamental mathematical understanding as well as recently acquired concepts and skills, combining problem-solving strategies with critical thinking skills.

Critical thinking skills enhanced by working on *Enrichment* exercises include classifying, comparing, sequencing, analyzing parts and whole, identifying patterns and relationships, induction (from specific to general), deduction (from general to specific), and spatial visualization.

One set of problems is provided for each chapter, to be assigned after the chapter has been completed. *Enrichment* exercises can be assigned while other students are working on the Chapter Review/Test, or while the class is working on subsequent chapters.

BLANK

CHAPTER 1 Numbers to 10

PROBLEM SOLVING
Thinking Skills

Solve.
Show your work.

1. Amy and Jill count the number of wheels on their toys. Who has more wheels on her toys?

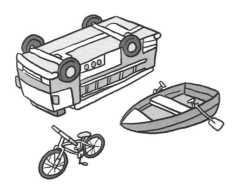

Amy's toys

Jill's toys

_____ has more wheels on her toys.

Enrichment 1A

Name: _____ Date: _____

2. Find the differences between the two pictures.
Color each difference that you find using a different color.
How many differences are there?

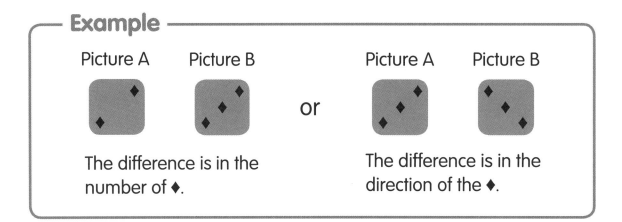

Example

Picture A   Picture B   Picture A   Picture B

or

The difference is in the   The difference is in the
number of ♦.   direction of the ♦.

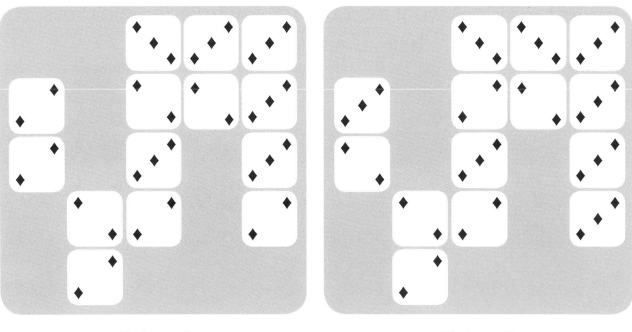

Picture A   Picture B

There are _____ differences.

Name: _____   Date: _____

PROBLEM SOLVING
Strategies

**Solve.
Show your work.**

— Example —

Joe is thinking of a number that is greater than 3 and less than 8.
What can the number be?

Draw a diagram or use another strategy **to help you.**

The number can be 4, 5, 6, or 7.

3. Megan has a ball with a number on it.
The number is greater than 2 but less than 7.
What can the number be?

The number can be _____, _____, _____, or _____.

Enrichment 1A   3

4. Jack is 3 years older than Hannah.
Hannah is 4 years old.
How old is Jack?

Jack is _____ years old.

5. Two years ago, Lori was 5 years old.
How old will Lori be 2 years from now?

Lori will be _____ years old.

6. These are groups of counters.

Draw them in the below to make a number pattern.

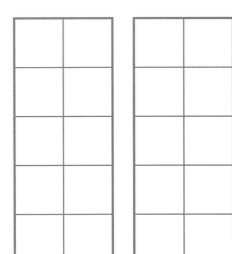 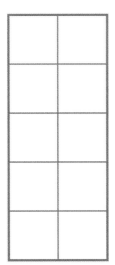 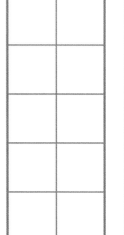

Name: _____ Date: _____

PROBLEM SOLVING
Exploration

Solve.
Show your work.

7. Chris is 10 years old.
Jess is more than 3 years old.
Pete is younger than Chris but older than Jess.
How old can Pete be?

Pete can be _____, _____, _____, _____,

or _____ years old.

8. Jackie wrote five numbers.

1 2 4 5 8

Trade some of the numbers so that the five numbers make a pattern.
Show two ways to do this.

Name: _____   Date: _____

 **Journal Writing**

Solve and tell why.

9.   0   1   3   6   9

Do the numbers form a pattern? _____
Tell your friend why.

10.   1   4   7   10

Do the numbers form a pattern? _____
Tell your friend why.

Correct the mistakes.
Write the correct sentences.

11.   1 more than 6 is 5.

_____

12.   1 less than 4 is 5.

_____

Enrichment 1A   7

Name: _____ Date: _____

 **Game**

Guess My Number!

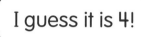

STEP 1 Each player writes a number between 0 and 10 on a piece of paper.

STEP 2 Player 1 guesses Player 2's number.

I guess it is 4!

STEP 3 Player 2 can say:
"My number is greater than your guess",
"My number is less than your guess", or "You are correct!"

My number is greater than your guess.

STEP 4 Player 1 scores 1 point for guessing the number correctly. If not, it is Player 2's turn to guess Player 1's number.

STEP 5 The game continues until Player 1 or Player 2 guesses the mystery number correctly.

> The player with the higher score after ten games wins!

Chapter 1 Numbers to 10

Number Bonds

Fill in the number bonds to make 6.
Use these numbers only once in each number bond.

0 1 2 3 4 5

1.
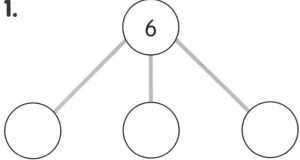

2.
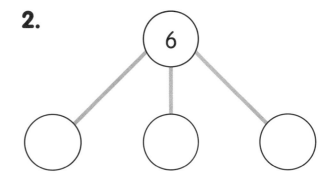

3.
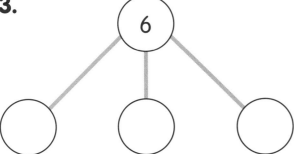

Enrichment 1A

Name: _____ Date: _____

Now use these numbers more than once in each number bond to make 6.

0 1 2 3 4 5

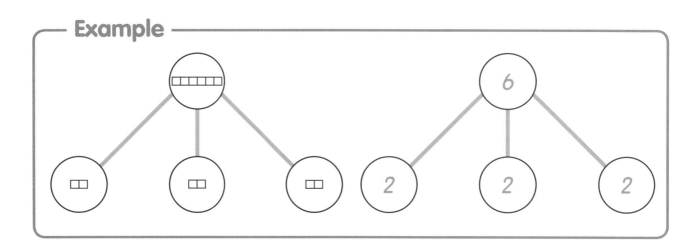

4.

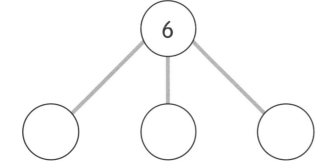

5.

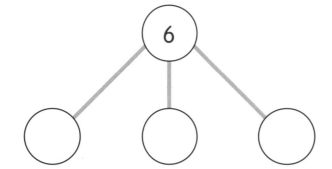

Name: _____ Date: _____

Fill in the number bonds to make 8.
Use these numbers only once in each number bond.

0 1 2 3 4 5 6 7

6.

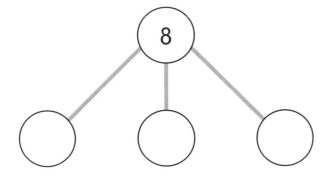

7.

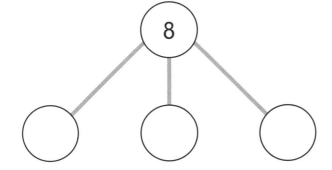

8.

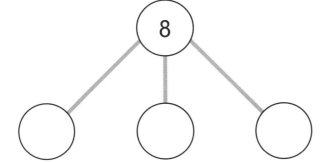

PROBLEM SOLVING Strategies

Fill in the ◯s with 1, 2, 3, 4, 5, and 6.
Use each number only once.

9. Each ◯—◯—◯ makes 9.

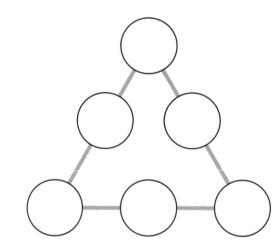

10. Each ◯—◯—◯ makes 10.

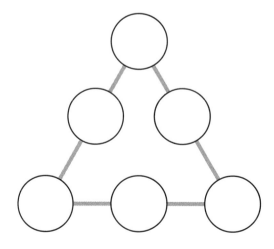

12 Chapter 2 Number Bonds

Fill in the missing numbers.

11. The numbers in each row and column make 9.
Find the missing numbers.

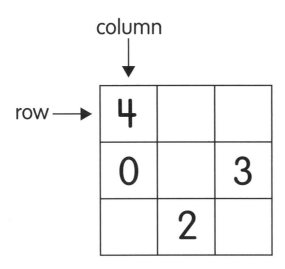

Solve.

12. Marta has one cat and some birds as pets.
The pets have 10 legs in all.
How many birds does Marta have?

Marta has _____ birds.

13. The numbers in each 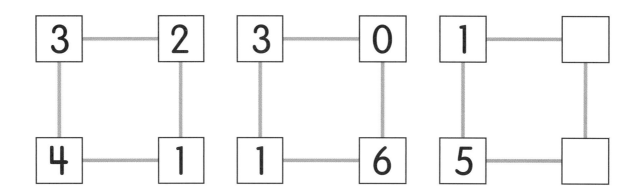 make a whole.
Find the whole. Then fill in the missing numbers.

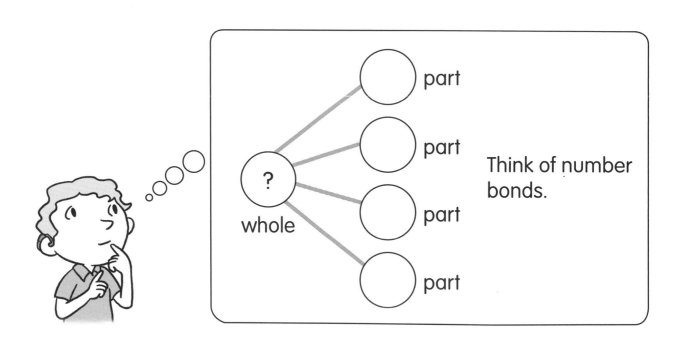

Name: _____ Date: _____

PROBLEM SOLVING
Exploration

Solve.
Show your work.

14. Farmer Annie has some 🐕 and 🐓 on her farm.
    The animals have 10 legs in all.
    How many 🐕 and 🐓 does she have?

There is more than one correct answer.

She has _____ 🐕 and _____ 🐓.

Enrichment 1A

Name: _____   Date: _____

15. Make number bonds for 5.
You can use a number more than once in a number bond.

Example

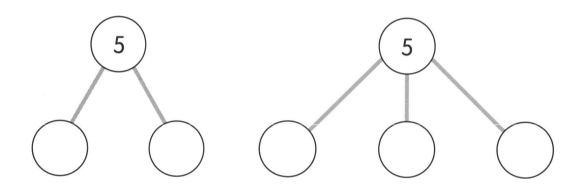

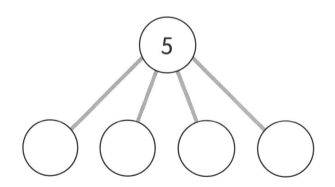

16   Chapter 2   Number Bonds

Name: _____   Date: _____

 Journal Writing

Solve and explain.

16. Can you make a number bond?
    Use each number only once.

    8   3   3   10   1

    Explain why or why not.

17. Write any five numbers to make two number bonds.
    Then complete the number bonds.

    _____ _____ _____ _____ _____

    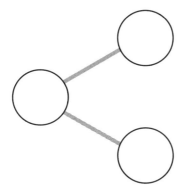   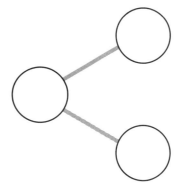

 **Game**

The Bond Connection!

Players: 2

STEP 1 Player 1 says a number between 5 and 10.

STEP 2 Player 2 writes all possible number bonds for that number.

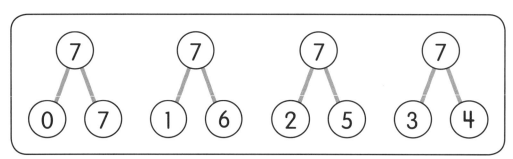

STEP 3 Player 2 scores 1 point for each correct number bond.

STEP 4 Players take turns saying numbers and writing number bonds.

> The player with the most points after ten games wins!

Name: _____ Date: _____

Addition Facts to 10

Fill in the blanks.

1. 2 more than 5 is _____.

2. _____ is 4 more than 2.

Solve.
Show your work.

3. An empty school bus picks up 4 children at Point A.
   It picks up 2 children at Point B.
   It picks up some more children at Point C.
   10 children are picked up in all.
   How many children are picked up at Point C?

   _____ children are picked up at Point C.

Enrichment 1A 19

Name: _____ Date: _____

Problem Solving Strategies

Solve.
Show your work.

4. Sue counts on from a number.
   Using 3 counts, she counts to 8.
   What is the number?

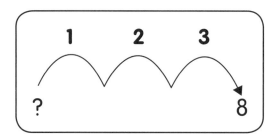

The number is _____.

Name: _____ Date: _____

5.

When you add 4 to me, the answer is 9.

What number am I?

I am _____.

6.

When you add 6 to me, the answer is 8.

What number am I?

I am _____.

Name: ______________________ Date: ____________

7. △ + □ = 9

△ + △ = □

△ = ________

□ = ________

8. Wendy has some stamps.
She gives 1 stamp to Christina and 3 stamps to Leon.
Wendy has 4 stamps left.
How many stamps did Wendy have at first?

Wendy had ________ stamps at first.

Name: _____ Date: _____

PROBLEM SOLVING
Exploration

Solve.
Show your work.

9. Shawn has more cherries than Will.
   They have 9 cherries in all.
   How many cherries does Will have?

   There is more than one correct answer.

   Will has _____ cherries.

10. Tracy gives 10 magnets to Jacob and Lin.
Jacob gets 2 more magnets than Lin.
How many magnets does Jacob get?

Magnets	Jacob	Lin	Jacob − Lin = 2?
10	9	1	9 − 1 = 8 (No)
10	8	2	8 − 2 = 6 (No)
⋮	⋮	⋮	⋮

Jacob gets _____ magnets.

Name: _____ Date: _____

 **Journal Writing**

**Solve.
Then write a story.**

11. Complete the number bond.
    Then write a story using the words.

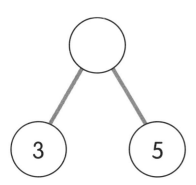

| farm | goats |
| chickens | how many |

Enrichment 1A   25

 Subtraction Facts to 10

Thinking Skills

Fill in the blanks.

1. 3 less than 8 is _____.

2. _____ is 2 less than 9.

**Solve.
Show your work.**

3. There were 8 boxes on a shelf.
   3 boxes were taken away on Monday.
   Some boxes were taken away on Tuesday.
   3 boxes are left.
   How many boxes were taken away on Tuesday?

   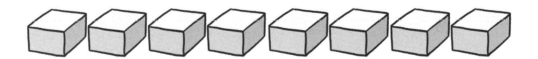

   _____ boxes were taken away on Tuesday.

PROBLEM SOLVING Strategies

Solve.
Show your work.

4. Mrs. Fisher has 8 apples.
   She gives 2 apples to each of her 2 sons.
   She eats 1 apple.
   How many apples does Mrs. Fisher have left?

   Mrs. Fisher has _____ apples left.

5. Amy is 5 years old.
   Her sister is 8 years old.
   How many years younger is Amy than her sister?
   One year ago, how many years younger was Amy than her sister?

   Amy is _____ years younger than her sister.

   One year ago, Amy was _____ years younger than her sister.

Enrichment 1A

Name: _____   Date: _____

6. Marcus thinks of two numbers.
   The numbers are greater than 0 but less than 10.
   When he adds the numbers, the answer is 7.
   When he subtracts one number from the other,
   the answer is 3.
   What are the two numbers?

   [?] + [?] = 7

   [?] − [?] = 3

   The two numbers are _____ and _____.

7. Caleb thinks of two numbers.
   The numbers are greater than 0 but less than 6.
   When he subtracts one number from the other,
   the answer is less than 2.
   What are the two numbers?

   There is more than one correct answer.

   The two numbers are _____ and _____.

Name: _____ Date: _____

PROBLEM SOLVING
Exploration

Solve.
Show your work.

8. Sally and Jing have 10 beads in all.
   Sally has fewer beads than Jing.
   How many beads can Sally have?

Sally	Jing	Total number of beads	Sally has fewer beads
1	9	10	Yes
2	8	10	Yes

There is more than one correct answer.

Sally could have _____, _____, _____,

or _____ beads.

Enrichment 1A 29

9. Bill and Jeff have 8 pencils in all.
In how many ways can the pencils be shared so that Jeff has 2 fewer pencils than Bill?

The pencils can be shared in _____ way(s).

Journal Writing

10. Tell your friend what the pattern in the picture is.

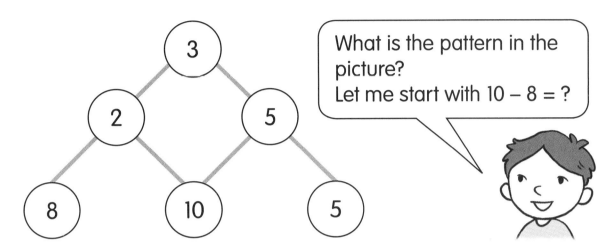

11. Fill in the ◯ to make a subtraction pattern.

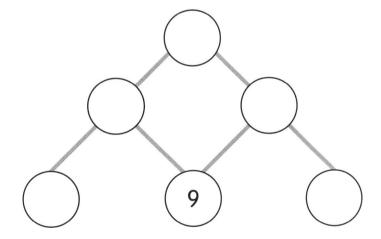

 **Game**

Subtract from 10!

Players: 2

STEP 1 Each player says a number that is between 0 and 5.

STEP 2 Players add the two numbers.

STEP 3 Then, players subtract the number in **STEP 2** from 10.

STEP 4 The first player to say the correct answer scores 1 point.

After 10 rounds, the player with the most points wins!

Chapter 4 Subtraction Facts to 10

Shapes and Patterns

Color.

1.

Look for the shapes that are the same.
Color them.
Use one color for each shape.

Enrichment 1A

Name: _____ Date: _____

**Look at the picture.
Then fill in the blanks.**

2.

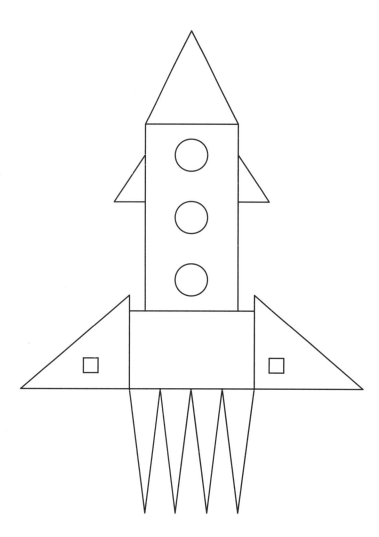

a. There are _____ circles.

b. There are _____ rectangles.

c. There are _____ squares.

d. There are _____ triangles.

e. The picture has _____ more circle(s) than squares.

Name: _____ Date: _____

**Find the shapes in the picture.
Then color.**

3.

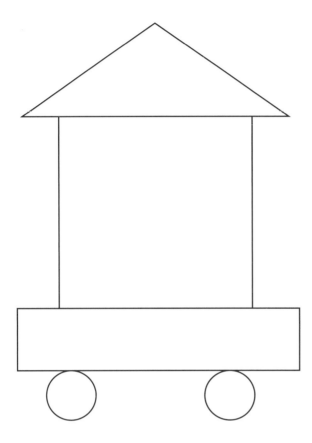

Color two circles blue.
Color one square green.
Color one rectangle orange.
Color one triangle purple.
Add a circle and a triangle to the picture.
Color both of them red.

4. Look at the triangles.

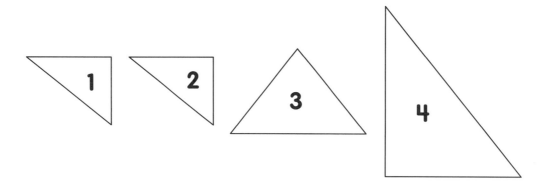

The triangles are cut and put together to form Picture A. Write the numbers in the correct triangles in Picture A.

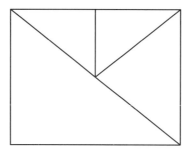

Picture A

Solve.

5. Sam uses cubes to make this shape. How many cubes does he use?

Sam uses _____ cubes.

PROBLEM SOLVING
Strategies

Complete the patterns.
Circle the shape that comes next.

6.   _____

7. 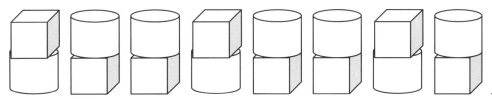 _____

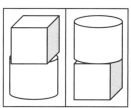

Circle the missing shape.

8.    _____

9.
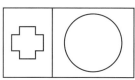

Enrichment 1A

Name: _____   Date: _____

**Complete the patterns.
Draw the next shape.
Then write the next number in the shape.**

10.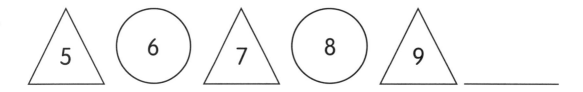

11.

Complete the pattern.

12. Fill in the last box with the correct number of ☾s.

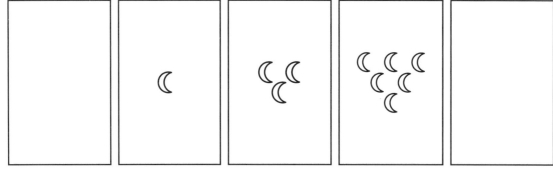

first   last

PROBLEM SOLVING
Exploration

Complete.

13.

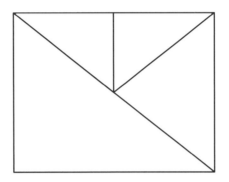

Trace and cut out these four triangles.
Arrange them to make a picture.
Arrange them again to make a different picture.

Enrichment 1A

Name: _____   Date: _____

 **Journal Writing**

Look at the shapes.
Fill in the blanks with *shape, size,* or *color*.

14.

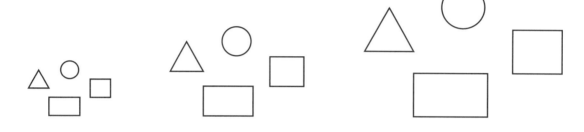

The shapes are sorted by _____.

15.

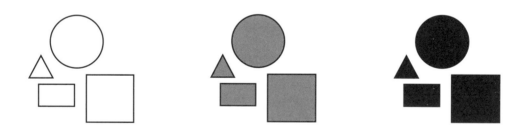

The shapes are sorted by _____.

40 Chapter 5 Shapes and Patterns

Name: _____ Date: _____

Look at the shapes.

16.

   a. Explain the pattern.

   _____

   _____

   _____

   _____

   b. What comes next?
   Circle the next shape in the pattern.

   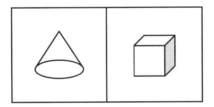

Ordinal Numbers and Position

Solve.

1. Choose a tree.
   Cross out (**X**) your tree.
   Then complete the sentence.

   a. I choose the _____ tree from the left.

   b. Circle the 5th tree from the right.

2.   **a.** Circle the boy right behind the 5th boy.

first　　　　　　　　　　　　　　　　　　last

b. The circled boy is now 3rd in line.
Cross out (**✗**) one or more children to show this.

How many children did you cross out? _____

3.   You sit with these friends in a classroom.
You are 3rd from Alex.
Eve sits behind you.
Felix sits next to you.
Jamie sits to your right.

Label the boxes to show where Alex, Eve, Felix, Jamie, and you sit.

Front [Alex] [   ] [   ] [   ] [   ]

Back [   ] [   ] [   ] [   ] [   ]

Name: _____ Date: _____

PROBLEM SOLVING
Strategies

Solve.
Show your work.

4. Kate is 3rd in line.
   Russell is 3rd from the end of the line.
   3 children stand between them.
   How many children are in the line?

   _____ children are in the line.

5. Some squares are placed in a row.
   A yellow square is 4th from the right.
   It is also 4th from the left.
   How many squares are in the row?

   _____ squares are in the row.

44 Chapter 6 Ordinal Numbers and Position

Name: _____ Date: _____

6. 9 children are in a line.
   Nelly is 4th from the front.
   Peter is last in line.
   How many children are between them?

   _____ children are between them.

7. Jimmy and Jay line up together to buy lunch.
   There are 7 people in line.
   2 people are in front of them.
   How many people are behind them?

   _____ people are behind them.

8. Doug, Allen, Hilary, Calvin, Evan, Freda, Basa, Max, and Ginger are standing in a line.

Doug Allen Hilary Calvin Evan Freda Basa Max Ginger

a. Who is the 7th person in line? _____

b. Some people left the line.
The person that was 7th in line is now 4th in line and is the only person between Calvin and Ginger. How many people left the line?

_____ people left the line.

c. Counting from the back, in what position is this person now?

This person is now the _____ person from the back.

Name: _____ Date: _____

9.   9 children are in a line.
Tammy is 6th in line.
Two children in front of Tammy leave the line.
One child behind Tammy also leaves the line.
How many children are in front of Tammy now?

_____ children are in front of Tammy now.

10.   There are 7 white beads arranged in a row.
The 5th bead is replaced with 2 red beads.
The first three beads are replaced with a green bead.
Two more yellow beads are then added to the back of the row.
How many beads are in the row now?

_____ beads are in the row now.

PROBLEM SOLVING
Exploration

Solve.
Show your work.

11. 8 children are in line to buy ice cream.
    Amy is behind Jamar.
    Kate is 5th from the back.
    Kate is between Jamar and Dawn.
    Draw pictures to show their positions in two ways.

Name: _____   Date: _____

 **Journal Writing**

True or false?

12. Write *true* or *false*.
If a statement is false, explain why it is wrong.
Draw pictures to help you.

    a. Trish is behind Sally.
       So, Sally is in front of Trish. _____

    b. There are 8 boats in a row.
       Boat A is 5th from the left.
       So, Boat A is 3rd from the right. _____

    c. Brian sits between Omar and Gina.
       Omar sits in front of Gina. _____

Write a story.

13. Five boys are sitting on a bench.

Jack   Louis   Steve   Brad   Henry

Write a story using some or all of the words.

| first | 4th | last | left | right |
| between | next | in front | behind | |

My story:
_____
_____
_____
_____
_____

CHAPTER 7 Numbers to 20

PROBLEM SOLVING
Thinking Skills

**Solve.
Show your work.**

1. Look at the picture.

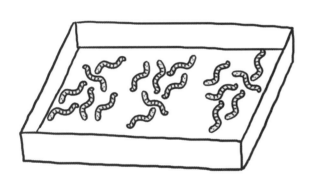 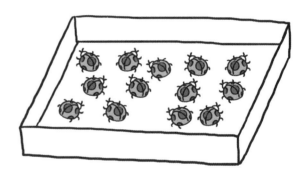

   a. Circle the box that has more.

   b. Cross out (**X**) some from the box with more so that it now has 2 less than the other box.
   How many did you cross out?

   I crossed out _____.

Enrichment 1A 51

2. Look at the picture.

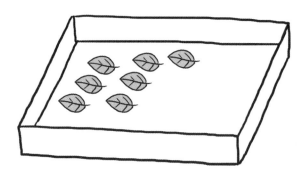 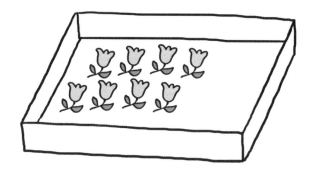

a. Circle the box that has less.

b. Draw some more in the box with less so that it now has 3 more than the other box.
How many more did you draw?

I drew _____ more.

Name: _____   Date: _____

3. Look at the picture.

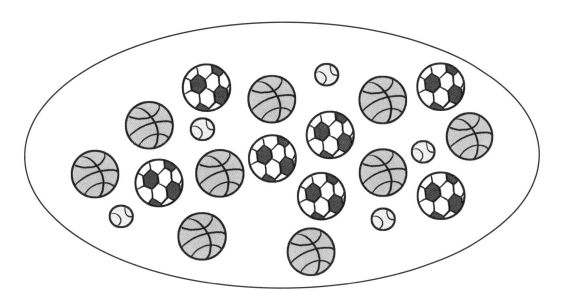

a. Check (✔) to show which type of ball has the most number of balls.

![Basketball]	![Soccer ball]	![Baseball]
Basketball	Soccer ball	Baseball

b. Which type of ball has the least
number of balls?   _____
Draw some more to make it 4 more than
the soccer balls.
How many more did you draw?

I drew _____ more.

Enrichment 1A   53

PROBLEM SOLVING
Strategies

Fill in the blanks.

4. 8 more than 5 is _____.

5. _____ is 5 more than 7.

6. 9 less than 18 is _____.

Solve.
Show your work.

7.
> I am a number between 8 and 20.
> When 5 is taken away from me and 8 is added back, I become the number 15.
> What number am I?

I am the number _____.

Name: _____ Date: _____

Complete the number pattern.

8. 7, _____, 11, _____, 15, 17, 19

9. _____, 6, 9, _____, 15

10. 4, 6, 9, 13, _____

11. 17, 16, _____, _____, 7, 2

Look at the pattern.

12. How many squares does the 6th layer have?

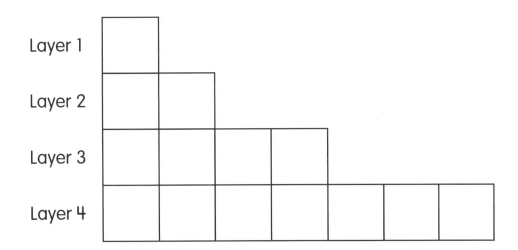

The 6th layer has _____ squares.

Enrichment 1A 55

13. Fill in the circles with the numbers 4, 5, 6, 7, 8, and 9.
Each ◯─◯─◯ makes 20.

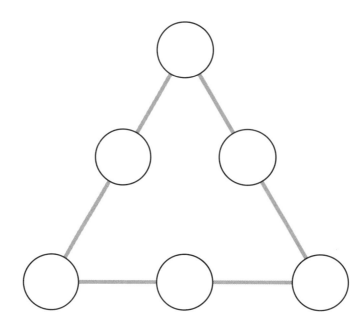

Name: _____   Date: _____

PROBLEM SOLVING
Exploration

Write sentences.

14. Use the words and numbers.
Write as many sentences as you can.
You may use the words and numbers more than once.

| 8 | more than | less than | 15 | 7 | is |

_____

_____

_____

_____

_____

_____

_____

_____

Enrichment 1A 57

Journal Writing

**Write *true* or *false*.
Explain your answer.**

15. 6 more than ♡ is 13.

♡ = 6 + 13 = 19

'More than' means 'add'.
So, I add 6 and 13.

_____

_____

16. 5 less than ✢ is 9.

✢ = 9 − 5 = 4

'Less than' means 'subtract'.
So, I subtract 5 from 9.

_____

_____

Name: _____ Date: _____

 # Addition and Subtraction Facts to 20

Thinking Skills

1. Fill in the blanks with 14, 13, and 7.

   a. _____ − _____ + _____ = 20

   b. _____ + _____ − _____ = 6

Solve.
Show your work.

2. 16 children are in a line.
   7 children leave the line.
   4 children join the line.
   How many children are in the line now?

   _____ children are in the line now.

Enrichment 1A 59

Name: _____   **Date:** _____

Solve.
Show your work.

3. $2 + 3 + 4 + 5 + 6 =$ _____

4. Find the value of ☐.

$$\triangle + \square + \bigcirc = 18$$

$$\square + \bigcirc = 11$$

$$\triangle = \bigcirc$$

The value of ☐ is _____.

Name: _____   Date: _____

PROBLEM SOLVING
Strategies

Solve.
Show your work.

5. Jill has some cards.
   She gives Ben 9 cards.
   She gives Kelly 4 cards.
   Jill has 2 cards left.
   How many cards did Jill have at first?

   Jill had _____ cards at first.

6. Greg thinks of two numbers.
   When he adds them, he gets 17.
   When he subtracts one from the other, he gets 9.
   What are the two numbers?

   A + B = 17
   A − B = 9
   What can A and B be?

   The two numbers are _____ and _____.

7. Ken buys a pack of pens.
He gives 8 pens to Josh.
Ken gives 3 pens to Gillian.
Ken finds 6 more pens.
Now Ken has 10 pens.
How many pens did Ken buy at first?

Ken bought _____ pens at first.

Name: _____ Date: _____

PROBLEM SOLVING
Exploration

Solve.

8. Write the number sentences.
Use three different numbers
from 5 to 15.

_____ + _____ − _____ = 12

_____ − _____ + _____ = 12

There is more than one correct answer.

9. Add 9 and 6.
Show three ways.
Use number bonds to help you.

9 + 6 = _____

10. Subtract 7 from 15.
Show two ways.
Use number bonds to help you.

15 − 7 = _____

Enrichment 1A 63

Name: _____ Date: _____

 **Journal Writing**

Write stories.

11. Write one addition story and one subtraction story. Use the numbers and words.

   | 5 | 9 | Brad | Sue | sold | how many |
   | apples | buys | 16 | more than | | |

   a. Addition story

   _____
   _____
   _____
   _____

   b. Subtraction story

   _____
   _____
   _____
   _____

64 **Chapter 8** Addition and Subtraction Facts to 20

Name: _____   Date: _____

Look at the problems Jack completed.
Find his mistakes.
Explain the mistakes Jack made.
Then solve the problems correctly.

12.   9
  − 6
  —
  15

13.   14
  − 8
  —
  14

Name: _____ Date: _____

Length

**Measure each line using paper clips.
Then write the length.**

The length of 1 paper clip is .

1a.

Line	Length 1 📎 = 1 unit
Line A _____	_____ units
Line B _____	_____ units
Line C _____	_____ units
Line D _____	_____ units

66 Chapter 9 Length

Name: _____   Date: _____

Read each sentence.
Check (✓) if the sentence is correct.

b.

Sentence	Check (✓) if correct
Line C is 1 paper clip longer than Line B.	
Line A is longer than Line C.	
Line B is longer than Line D.	
Line A is as long as Line D.	
Line B is the longest.	
The lengths of Line A, Line C, and Line D add up to 10 paper clips.	

Complete.

c. Draw a line that is one paper clip longer than Line B.

d. Draw a line that is two paper clips shorter than Line D.

Enrichment 1A

2. Look at the picture.
   Fill in the blanks.

Andy   Britney   Joel   Darlene

a. _____ is the next tallest after Darlene.

b. _____ is taller than Joel but shorter than Andy.

Complete. Write *shorter* or *taller*.

c. Darlene is _____ than Andy.

Andy is _____ than Joel.

So, Joel is _____ than Darlene.

Name: _____ Date: _____

**Look at the picture.
Fill in the blanks.**

3.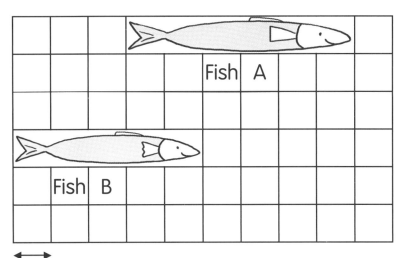

1 unit

a. Fish A is about _____ units long.

b. Fish A is about _____ unit(s) _____ than Fish B.

Name: _____ Date: _____

PROBLEM SOLVING
Strategies

**Solve.
Show your work.**

4. The length of a pencil is 12 units.
    The length of a crayon is shown.

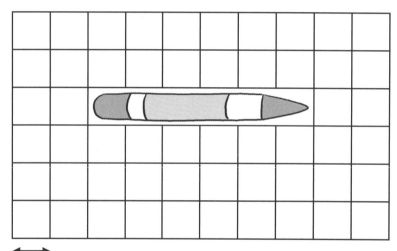

1 unit

If the pencil and the crayon are put together end to end, what is the total length?

The total length is about _____ units.

70 Chapter 9 Length

Name: _____ Date: _____

5. Five erasers are placed in a row.
Each eraser is 3 units long.
There is 1 unit between every two erasers.
What is the total length from the first eraser to the last?

The total length is _____ units.

6. Eleanor draws nine dots in a row.
The dots are 2 units apart from one another.
How far is the last dot from the first?

The last dot is _____ units from the first dot.

7. There are 6 marks along a line.
The marks are 3 units apart from one another.
How far is the 2nd mark from the 5th mark?

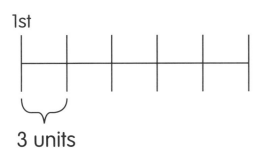

The 2nd mark is _____ units from the 5th mark.

Enrichment 1A

PROBLEM SOLVING
Exploration

Solve.
Show your work.

8. An ant crawls from A to B along the lines.

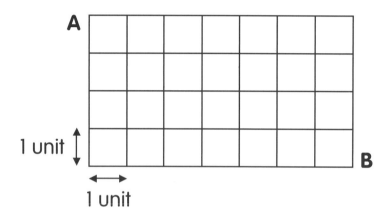

a. Trace the shortest path from A to B.

b. The shortest path from A to B is _____ units long.

c. Draw three paths that are 6 units longer than the shortest path.

Name: _____ Date: _____

Journal Writing

Find the mistake.
Then write the correct sentence.

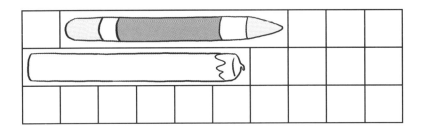

9. Jackie says that the crayon is longer than the candle.

_____

_____

10. The length of a pen is about 9 paper clips.
The length of a pencil is about 2 sticks.
The pen is as long as the pencil.

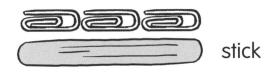 stick

_____

_____

Name: _____ Date: _____

11. Look at the picture.
Explain how you know that the pencil is shorter than the ribbon.
Use **units** in your answer.

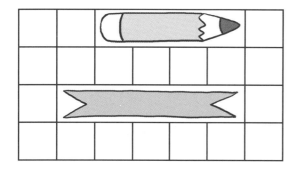

_____

_____

_____

Answers

Chapter 1

1. Thinking skill: Comparing
   Solution: Jill
2. Thinking skill: Comparing
   Solution: 5
3. Strategy: Use a diagram
   Solution: 3, 4, 5, or 6
4. Strategy: Use a diagram
   Solution: 7
5. Strategy: Use a diagram
   Solution: 9
6. Strategy: Look for patterns
   Solution:
   Accept 1, 3, 5, 7, 9; 9, 7, 5, 3, 1
7. 5, 6, 7, 8, or 9
8. Accept 1, 2, 3, 4, 5; 2, 4, 6, 8, 10
9. No. (correct pattern should be: +1, +2, +3, +4)
10. Yes. (pattern is: +3, +3, +3)
11. Accept 1 less than 6 is 5; 1 more than 5 is 6.
12. Accept 1 more than 4 is 5; 1 less than 5 is 4.

Chapter 2

1. Thinking skill: Analyzing parts and whole
   Solution:
   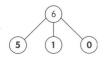
2. Thinking skill: Analyzing parts and whole
   Solution:
   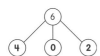
3. Thinking skill: Analyzing parts and whole
   Solution:
   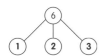
4. Thinking skill: Analyzing parts and whole
   Solution:
   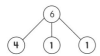
5. Thinking skill: Analyzing parts and whole
   Solution:

6. Thinking skill: Analyzing parts and whole
   Solution:

7. Thinking skill: Analyzing parts and whole
   Solution:
   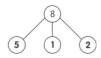
8. Thinking skill: Analyzing parts and whole
   Solution:
   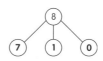
9. Strategy: Guess and check/Trial and error
   Solution:
   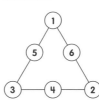
10. Strategy: Guess and check/Trial and error
    Solution:

11. Strategy: Guess and check/Trial and error
    Solution:

4	1	4
0	6	3
5	2	2

Enrichment 1A

12. Strategy: Guess and check/Trial and error
    Solution: Marta has 3 birds.
13. Strategy: Look for patterns
    Solution: Answers vary. Accept any two one-digit numbers that make 10 when added to 1 and 5.
    For example, 1, 3.
14.
    Accept 1 dog, 3 chickens; 2 dogs, 1 chicken
15. Number bond with 2 parts: Accept 0, 5; 1, 4; 2, 3
    Number bonds with 3 parts: Answers vary.
    Number bonds with 4 parts: Answers vary.
16. No. The parts do not make a whole.
17. Answers vary.

Chapter 3

1. Thinking skill: Comparing
   Solution: 7
2. Thinking skill: Comparing
   Solution: 6
3. Thinking skill: Analyzing parts and whole
   Solution:
   4 + 2 + 4 = 10
   4 children are picked up at Point C.
4. Strategy: Use a diagram
   Solution:
   5 + 3 = 8
   The number is 5.
5. Strategy: Use a diagram
   Solution: 5
6. Strategy: Use a diagram
   Solution: 2
7. Strategy: Use a diagram
   Solution:

   △ + ▢ = 9
   △ + △ = ▢
   △ + △ + △ = 9
   So, △ = 3
   ▢ = 6

8. Strategy: Work backward
   Solution:
   4 + 3 + 1 = 8
   Wendy had 8 stamps at first.
9. Accept 0; 1; 2; 3; 4
10.

Magnets	Jacob	Lin	Jacob − Lin = 2?
10	9	1	9 − 1 = 8 (No)
10	8	2	8 − 2 = 6 (No)
10	7	3	7 − 3 = 4 (No)
10	6	4	6 − 4 = 2 (Yes)

Jacob gets 6 magnets.

11.
    Answers vary.

Chapter 4

1. Thinking skill: Comparing
   Solution: 5
2. Thinking skill: Comparing
   Solution: 7
3. Thinking skill: Analyzing parts and whole
   Solution:
   3 + 3 = 6
   8 − 6 = 2
   2 boxes were taken away on Tuesday.
4. Strategy: Use a diagram
   Solution:

   8 − 2 − 2 − 1 = 3
   Mrs. Fisher has 3 apples left.
5. Strategy: Use a diagram
   Solution:
   8 − 5 = 3
   Amy is 3 years younger than her sister.
   Amy was 3 years younger than her sister.

6. Strategy: Guess and check/Trial and error
   Solution:
   List pairs of numbers that make 7 first.
   Then subtract the two possible numbers to get 3.

Number 1	Number 2	After adding	After subtracting	Correct
6	1	7	5	No
5	2	7	3	Yes
4	3	7	1	No

   The two numbers are 5 and 2.

7. Strategy: Guess and check/Trial and error
   Answers vary.
   The two numbers are less than 6.
   So, 5 is the greatest number and 1 is the smallest number.

Number 1	Number 2	Difference	Difference is less than 2
5	5	0	Yes
5	4	1	Yes
5	3	2	No

   Accept: 5, 5; 5, 4; 4, 4; 4, 3; 3, 3; 3, 2; 2, 2; 2, 1; 1, 1

8. List pairs of numbers that make 10 first.
   1 and 9 make 10.
   1 is 8 fewer than 9.

Sally	Jing	Total number of beads	Sally has fewer beads
1	9	10	Yes
2	8	10	Yes
3	7	10	Yes
4	6	10	Yes
5	5	10	No

   1, 2, 3, or 4

9. List the pairs of numbers that make 8 first.
   Bill has more pencils.

Bill	Jeff	Total number of pencils	Jeff has 2 fewer pencils
7	1	8	No (7 − 1 = 6)
6	2	8	No (6 − 2 = 4)
5	3	8	Yes (5 − 3 = 2)

   One way. Bill has 5 pencils and Jeff has 3 pencils.

10. 10 − 8 = 2
    10 − 5 = 5
    5 − 2 = 3
    This is a subtraction pattern.

11. Answers vary.

Chapter 5

1. Thinking skill: Classifying
   Solution:

   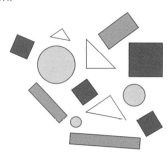

   Notice that squares are rectangles; if students had colored squares and rectangles using the same color, they are also correct.

2. Thinking skill: Classifying, Comparing
   Solution:
   a. 3   b. 2
   c. 2   d. 9
   e. 1

3. Thinking skill: Classifying
   Solution:

   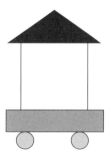

4. Thinking skill: Comparing
   Solution:

   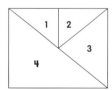

5. Thinking skill: Spatial visualization
   Solution: 12

6. Strategy: Look for patterns
   Solution:

Enrichment 1A

7. Strategy: Look for patterns
   Solution:

8. Strategy: Look for patterns
   Solution:

9. Strategy: Look for patterns
   Solution:

10. Strategy: Look for patterns
    Solution:

11. Strategy: Look for patterns
    Solution:

12. Strategy: Look for patterns
    Solution:

13. Answers vary.
14. size
15. color
16. a. 1 cone, 1 cube, 2 cones, 1 cube, 3 cones, 1 cube
    b.

Chapter 6

1. Thinking skill: Sequencing
   Solution:
   a. Answers vary.
   b. [fifth tree from right circled]

2. Thinking skill: Sequencing
   Solution:
   a. [6th boy circled]
   b. [Cross out first 3 boys]
      3 children

3. Thinking skill: Sequencing
   Solution:

Front	Alex	Felix	Me	Jamie	
Back			Eve		

4. Strategy: Use a diagram
   Solution:

   9 children are in the line.

5. Strategy: Use a diagram
   Solution:

   7 squares are in the row.

6. Strategy: Use a diagram
   Solution:

   4 children are between them.

7. Strategy: Use a diagram
   Solution:
   1   2   3   4   5   6   7
           Jimmy Jay
   3 people are behind them.

8. Strategy: Use a diagram
   Solution:
   a. Basa
   b. 4 people left the line.
   c. 2nd

9. Strategy: Use a diagram
   Solution:
   Before: Tammy
                            ↓
               x x x x x x x x x
   After: Tammy
                            ↓
               x x x x x x
   3 children are in front of Tammy now.

10. Strategy: Use a diagram
    Solution:
    G W R R W W Y Y
    8 beads are in the row now.

11. _ _ D K J A _ _

    _ _ A J K D _ _

12. a. True
    b. False

                A
    x x x x x x x x
    If Boat A is 5th from the left, it will be 4th from the right.
    c. False

    O   G
    B   or   B
    G   O

    In both cases, Omar is not in front of Gina.

13. Answers vary.

Chapter 7

1. Thinking skill: Comparing
   Solution:
   a. [box on the left circled]
   b. 7

2. Thinking skill: Comparing
   Solution:
   a. [box on the left circled]
   b. 4

3. Thinking skill: Classifying, Comparing
   Solution:
   a.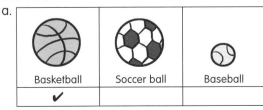
   b. Baseball, 6

4. Strategy: Use a diagram
   Solution: 13

5. Strategy: Use a diagram
   Solution: 12

   | 5 | 6 | 7 | 8 | 9 | 10 | 11 | ⑫ | 13 | 14 | 15 |

6. Strategy: Use a diagram
   Solution: 9

   | ⑨ | 10 | 11 | 12 | 13 | 14 | 15 | 16 | 17 | 18 | 19 |

7. Strategy: Work backward
   Solution:
   15 − 8 + 5 = 12
   I am the number 12.

8. Strategy: Look for patterns
   Solution:
   9, 13 (pattern of adding 2)

9. Strategy: Look for patterns
   Solution:
   3, 12 (pattern of adding 3)

10. Strategy: Look for patterns
    Solution:
    18 (pattern is: +2, +3, +4, +5)

11. Strategy: Look for patterns
    Solution:
    14, 11 (pattern is: −2, −3, −4, −5)

12. Strategy: Look for patterns
    Solution:
    Layer 1: 1
    Layer 2: 1 + 1 = 2
    Layer 3: 2 + 2 = 4
    Layer 4: 4 + 3 = 7
    Layer 5: 7 + 4 = 11
    Layer 6: 11 + 5 = 16
    The 6th layer has <u>16</u> squares.

13. Strategy: Look for patterns, Guess and check
    Solution:
    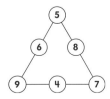

14. Answers vary. Accept:
    7 more than 8 is 15.
    8 more than 7 is 15.
    7 less than 15 is 8.
    8 less than 15 is 7.

15. False.
    13 − 6 = 7
    Check: 6 + 7 = 13
    ♡ = 7

16. False.
    9 + 5 = 14
    Check: 14 − 5 = 9
    ✚ = 14

Chapter 8

1. Thinking skill: Analyzing parts and whole
   Solution:
   a. 14 − 7 + 13 = 20
   b. 7 + 13 − 14 = 6

2. Thinking skill: Analyzing parts and whole
   Solution:
   16 − 7 + 4 = 13
   13 children are in the line now.

3. Thinking skill: Analyzing parts and whole
   Solution:
   2 + 3 + 4 + 5 + 6
   (grouped as 8 and 8)
   = 4 + 8 + 8
   = 20

4. Thinking skill: Analyzing parts and whole, Identifying patterns & relationships
   Solution:
   △ + 11 = 18
   △ = ○ = 7
   □ + 7 = 11
   □ = 4
   The value of □ is 4.

5. Strategy: Work backward
   Solution:
   2 + 4 + 9 = 15
   Jill had 15 cards at first.

6. Strategy: Restate the problem, Simplify the problem
   Solution:
   A + B = 17
   A − B = 9

List all possibilities	Difference	Is the difference 9?
16, 1	15	✗
15, 2	13	✗
14, 3	11	✗
13, 4	9	✓

   The two numbers are 4 and 13.

7. Strategy: Work backward
   Solution:
   10 − 6 + 3 + 8 = 15
   Ken bought 15 pens at first.

8. Answers vary.
   For example,
   14 + 6 − 8 = 12
   13 − 6 + 5 = 12

9. Method 1
   9 + 6 = 15
   (1) (5)
   9 + 1 = 10
   10 + 5 = 15

   Method 2
   9 + 6 = 15
   (5) (4)
   4 + 6 = 10
   5 + 10 = 15

   Method 3
   9 + 6 = 15
   (4)(5) (5)(1)
   5 + 5 = 10
   4 + 10 + 1 = 15

10. Method 1
    15 − 7 = 8
    (5)(10)
    10 − 7 = 3
    5 + 3 = 8

    Method 2
    15 − 7 = 8
    (8)(7)
    7 − 7 = 0
    8 + 0 = 8

11. Answers vary.
    For example,
    a. Brad buys 5 apples and Sue buys 9. How many apples do they buy altogether?
    b. Sue buys 16 apples. She gives 5 to Brad. How many apples does she have left?
12. Subtract, not add. 9 − 6 = 3
13. 8 ones cannot be subtracted from 4 ones.
    14 − 8 = 6

Chapter 9

1. Thinking skill: Comparing
   Solution:
   a.
Line	Length 1 📎 = 1 unit
Line A	4 units
Line B	2 units
Line C	3 units
Line D	4 units

   b.
Sentence	Check (✔) if correct
Line C is 1 paper clip longer than Line B.	✔
Line A is longer than Line C.	✔
Line B is longer than Line D.	
Line A is as long as Line D.	✔
Line B is the longest.	
The lengths of Line A, Line C and Line D add up to 10 paper clips.	

   c. [Draw a 9 cm line.]
   d. [Draw a 6 cm line.]

2. Thinking skill: Sequencing, Comparing
   Solution:
   a. Andy
   b. Britney
   c. taller; taller; shorter

3. Thinking skill: Comparing
   Solution:
   a. 6
   b. 1; longer

4. Strategy: Use a diagram
   Solution:
   12 + 6 = 18
   The total length is about 18 units.

5. Strategy: Use a diagram, Look for patterns
   Solution:
   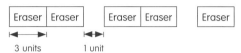
   3 + 3 + 1 + 3 + 3 + 1 + 3 = 17
   The total length is 17 units.

6. Strategy: Use a diagram
   Solution:

   2 + 2 + 2 + 2 + 2 + 2 + 2 + 2 = 16
   The last dot is 16 units from the first dot.

7. Strategy: Use a diagram
   Solution:

   3 + 3 + 3 = 9
   The 2nd mark is 9 units from the 5th mark.

8. a. Answers vary.
      Accept all drawings that are 11 units long.
   b. 11
   c. Answers vary.

9. The crayon is 6 units long.
   The candle is also 6 units long.
   Jackie says that the crayon is as long as the candle.

10. 3 paper clips = 1 stick
    9 paper clips (3 + 3 + 3) = 3 sticks
    The length of the pen is 3 sticks long.
    The pen is longer than the pencil.

11. The pencil is 4 units long.
    The ribbon is 5 units long.
    The pencil is shorter than the ribbon.

BLANK